ABORTION

Pauline Harmange

ABORTION

a personal story,
a political choice

translated by
Caitlin O'Neil

SCRIBE
Melbourne • London

Scribe Publications
18–20 Edward St, Brunswick, Victoria 3056, Australia
2 John St, Clerkenwell, London, WC1N 2ES, United Kingdom
3754 Pleasant Ave, Suite 100, Minneapolis, Minnesota 55409, USA

First published in French as *Avortée: Une histoire intime de l'IVG*
by Éditions Daronnes 2022
Published in English by Scribe 2023

Copyright © Éditions Daronnes, 2022
Translation arranged through Julie Finidori Agency
Translation copyright © Caitlin O'Neil 2023

Typeset in Portait Text by the publishers

Printed and bound in the UK by CPI Group (UK) Ltd,
Croydon CR0 4YY

Scribe is committed to the sustainable use of natural resources and
the use of paper products made responsibly from those resources.

Scribe acknowledges Australia's First Nations peoples as the
traditional owners and custodians of this country, and we pay
our respects to their elders, past and present.

978 1 761380 02 0 (Australian edition)
978 1 915590 00 8 (UK edition)
978 1 957363 29 5 (US edition)
978 1 922586 95 7 (ebook)

Catalogue records for this book are available from the
National Library of Australia and the British Library.

scribepublications.com.au
scribepublications.co.uk
scribepublications.com

For Soriya, who healed me with our first
murmured exchanges.

And for my sister, who repeated in the dark, her hand
in mine, the refrain from a cherished song:
'In two years, we'll both laugh about this.'
(From 'Palladium', by Brigitte)

CONTENTS

CONTENTS

FOREWORD

It's an occupational hazard: when I had my abortion, I knew very early on that I would want and need to write about everything that had happened. Everything happening still. I needed time to understand what it was that I had (a personal story interspersed with reflections) and what I could not do (use this book as a personal journal). It wasn't easy because for me, abortion landed precisely on this razor's edge. So intimate, so deeply emotional, but also so political in reach.

Another occupational hazard is that I often wonder what story is being told, and especially *why* it is being told.

When I first began working on this text, only a few months after my abortion, I was furious. Furious that I was so unhappy and also alone. I thought that my loneliness was due to a singularity of situation. That no one else had ever experienced what I was experiencing — and that there wasn't room for my experience. I found the discourses on abortion incredibly binary. My stomach clenched when I watched anti-choice protests pass by, and my heart tightened when I thought of the first-hand stories gathered by feminists as a counterbalance. None of that was true, I said to myself, wrapped in my pain.

I wanted people to speak honestly about abortion; I was deceived by the crushing loneliness that was painfully difficult for me to navigate. Several months after the fact, I learned that before we speak more truthfully, even before that, we have to speak louder.

Even today, no one wants to listen to women who have had abortions. What happens in our bodies and in our minds when we choose to no longer be pregnant is still too distasteful, too sordid, and too shameful. They'd rather we just shut up. But it's no longer fashionable to tell women to shut up, so if it's truly necessary for us to open our mouths, then they'll allow us to speak quietly, eyes locked on the ground, and without going into too much detail, if you'd be so kind.

I was a feminist before my abortion. When I wasn't healing, emotionally, from the pain of the abortion, but I nevertheless felt obligated to tell everyone, 'I'm fine, thanks', it took a while for me to identify what was underlying my response. I wasn't fine, but you don't say that, miserable woman! You don't say — in a world where so many women can't freely access abortions, in a world where at any given moment we know that this right can be taken from us — that you've had an abortion and ugh, frankly, it wasn't great.

I confused my loyalty to feminism, which had given me so much and which suddenly felt so limiting under the circumstances, with what was really at play: the silence imposed on women who do what they want. When I said, 'I'm fine' — when actually I wanted to cry — it wasn't my feminism that was betraying me: it was the law of silence that perpetuates taboo. I didn't want to give those awful people even one more drop of fuel to add to their fire; I wanted to be worthy of this right that was so hard won and which is constantly being dragged back up for debate. It took some time for me to understand that it wasn't feminism that was causing me to act like this. It's not that I was being told to be fine; it's that I was heeding the patriarchal command to fit inside a single box and not venture outside it. Because with abortion, like so many other subjects of debate that largely affect oppressed minorities, there is no room for complexity.

How better to honour the women who have fought for abortion rights, those who are still fighting around the world, those who have suffered from its illegality, those who still suffer from its limitations, than to continue to talk about it? I'm a feminist, but I have never had to fight for my right to access abortion. So, I grew up naively (I believe) thinking that here in France, at least, it was almost a non-subject. A right like any other, a mundane procedure barely worthy of notice. In fact, it's the opposite. It's still a subject that sparks incomprehension, hate, and loneliness.

I'm writing my story to combat this loneliness, to join the chorus of voices speaking up about abortion. I'm writing for the young woman I was when I typed 'personal abortion story' into the internet search engine, and for the one who will do the same thing today. Who will, like I did, land on a disguised anti-choice propaganda website, before finally accessing information that is objective, medically informed, and honest.

I've spent so much time talking about my abortion to other women, head held high, so much time recognising my sisters in this life experience. I'm writing this to say everything that the burden of taboo prevented me from understanding earlier, slowing my healing process. To bring us closer to the light.

INTRODUCTION

It was a beautiful December day, and we were returning home from a weekend with friends. When we checked the mail, there was an announcement. The senders of the news were people I love dearly, even though we don't often see them. We had shared commonalities that I appreciated: they also got married without caring too much about tradition, they also love Stephen King, LEGO, and Arctic Monkeys. Family, you know? This was my first time receiving an announcement like this, proof that, get ready, I was entering the period of life when people my age were having children. Because here was our warning: in seven months there would be a brand-new baby on this planet.

My belly made the calculations before my head did. I gasped, got dizzy. It could have been me. At the same moment, give or take a few days, it could have been me, my baby bump, and my baby. But it was not me, because more than a month earlier, I'd had my abortion.[1]

When my husband's back was turned, seized with rage and jealousy, I threw the announcement in the trash. Several months later, he asked me where that glittery card was, containing its good news. I looked him straight in the eye and told him, feigning innocence: 'I don't know, maybe it got lost, or thrown out accidentally. It happens.' I preferred to lie to him than acknowledge my action, so childish and cruel, of throwing that happiness in the trash. The shame.

Time passed, and I got really good at evading. I avoided encounters with friends who were pregnant, and that's how I began to realise they were truly everywhere. I'd already cancelled one date with a university friend who was expecting a baby, but that one was understandable: I was still bleeding from the after-effects of the abortion. Several months later, when the happy future parents (whose announcement I'd thrown out) came to visit, I fled again. How was I supposed to share my personal space — that had seen me asleep on the couch, knocked out by some nameless fatigue, that had heard me groaning with pain during my abortion, that had smelled the blood I'd washed off afterwards — with a pregnant woman? With

---

1 Two years later, I recalculated with my head this time. I'd been completely mistaken, more than six weeks off: that pregnancy had never mirrored mine.

her round belly, her shiny hair, her own fatigue, as well, of course. Her body full, and mine empty. I left, my whole body in knots.

I struggle to find the words to describe this ugly mix of feelings. Why this overwhelming sadness? Hadn't I fully thought through this decision? I stayed on the lookout for the first terrible signs of regret. I told myself that this pain must be proof that I was kicking myself, even subconsciously, for my abortion. That if I had it to do over again, I would have gone the other route. Today, I understand that I had to get to a place where this strange grief could coexist alongside the certainty, which has never left me, of having made the best decision possible.

I can look back gently now on the bruised woman I was. I was a bit of a brute, no doubt, and very selfish, too. I needed to protect myself. Not from pregnant women and new mothers, not from their happiness and their worries, but from this raw wound that laid me out flat despite my certainties. In the pit of my stomach, envy hardened me, filled me with spitefulness, because I did everything in my power to ignore it. After my abortion, I tried to prevent these versions of myself from taking root, infecting and rotting, while I worked to put myself back together.

I wasn't yet completely back to myself by July, when we received the second announcement, this time for the birth. But I smiled at this one. I looked at it for a long time, my heart pinched, no longer tight, just exhausted. And instead of throwing it out, I tucked it behind some other cards. That was eighteen months ago, and I know: that was the moment that healing began. Tucking away instead of throwing out, knowing that one day there would be a desire to rejoice, knowing in that instant that

one day

it would be okay.

PAIN AND ENVY

The story begins in October. Fall was unfolding and under its incessant storms, I was job-hunting after finally graduating and leaving the halls of the university. I was living with my husband, who was alternating between short temp jobs and long periods of unemployment, in a small apartment full of charm. That's real-estate code for a place that's poorly insulated, poorly equipped, poorly maintained, but with the benefit of a small, pretty, private garden. We counted our blessings on our fingers: we loved each other very much, we had a roof over our heads, we had a cat. Other than that, we were poor and sad, in greater or lesser degrees depending on the season: sometimes poor enough that we wondered how much longer we could pay the rent, sometimes sad enough that we had to take medication. We often reassured each other that *the bad days will end*. All our dreams were packed into these five small words. Real adults, I told myself, have goals and five-year plans to achieve them. We only allowed ourselves dreams, punctuated by uncertainty.

One failure to acknowledge from that time is that as the offspring of two upper-middle-class professionals, I should have continued to climb the social ladder, and I should have been sufficiently well-off for the question of money to only be rhetorical. But in France, things have been stagnating for the last twenty or thirty years, and the lies of living in a meritocracy are no longer believable. For the young adults of my generation, disillusionment spills out over every lunchtime chat. From those who've never had a shot at the famous 'equal opportunity', and others who've never had the privilege of accessing many of the opportunities to even maintain, much less improve, their social position. All in all, so many of us have been hung out to dry.

At the age I was then, my mother already had a full-time job, a car, a line of credit, a house, and a child on the way. The exact opposite of my reality. At the time, I was stuck in a studio apartment that I couldn't leave because my situation had become even worse since we'd moved in.

I was, admittedly, partially responsible for this failure. I was slow to finish my degree, and then once I did, I wasn't very diligent in my job hunt. I was picky because I don't care much for capitalism, or productivity, or rate of return, or getting up in the morning. I like to write, which at that moment of my life, I didn't even dare admit to myself, didn't even entertain it as a life choice. So I dragged my feet on getting a job. That doesn't help with poverty. I can tell myself all I want (because it's what I believe) that today's system of labour is violent and alienating, but that doesn't make me any less poor or discontent living in it. Only (barely) more in control.

So there I was in my third month of fruitless job searching, struggling to pay my share of the bills when suddenly, in the middle of general fatigue, sore breasts, and a wickedly bad mood, my phone pinged. It was my period tracking app telling me: 'Your period is late.' I was already aware, because I'm as regular as a clock. Thirty-one days, thirty-two tops. I'd like to say that a part of me already knew the truth, because that would be a little mystical and very 'modern witch'. The truth of it, though, is that the symptoms of early pregnancy can be exactly the same as those of PMS. Days three and four of being late, I rationalised. Tired and depressed, naturally, between unemployment and my period coming, since I didn't have much of anything to do, I began taking early-afternoon naps. I'm used to my breasts swelling and becoming hard and tender, and having to apply anti-inflammatory cream to them in order to sleep. I felt queasy and told myself, like everyone I'd talked to about it, that my period had to be coming. I had an IUD, dammit. Day five, though, permanent doubt settled in. What if I was pregnant?

No, not me.

I'd done everything to prevent it. Well, I liked to tell myself, 'I did everything to prevent it', when in reality, I'd just had a T made out of plastic and copper placed inside me so I could have sex without having to think about it. The penis in question would have had to stay far away from my vagina in order for me to have done *everything* to avoid it. A little voice jeered inside me: *Sucks to be you!* I didn't know yet, in that moment, that 72% of abortions in France are performed on women who were using contraception when they got pregnant,[i] that I wasn't alone in being unlucky. That there were, in fact, thousands, millions, of us.

Two more days passed, and my period still hadn't arrived. I decided to do a test that Monday morning, at the end of a feverish week of waiting. The night before, I'd placed the little cardboard box next to the toilet. Exhausted, I went back over the signs, again and again. Tender breasts, fatigue ... and the blood that just wouldn't come. I still wanted to sleep, but there was no way I was doing the test alone after my husband left for work. So as soon as the alarm rang, I got up, soaked the stick in the morning's first urine and set it face-down before starting the timer. Each racing heartbeat thudded in my chest. It was inescapable and interminable. Three minutes later, the test face-up in my shaking hand, I let out a joyless laugh.

I'm pregnant. Hahaha.

First came indescribable relief. I *can* get pregnant. My ovaries are functional, my uterus can be hospitable, this possibility exists in my body. I took this knowledge and tucked it away warmly, somewhere near the hole that would soon open within me. Confusingly, I felt that this revelation would serve me well in the future — and it's true that several years later, I did tell myself that if I'd already been pregnant once with this man, then maybe I could do it again. A lot of good that knowledge did me then, though. Setting the results aside, I collapsed in tears in my husband's arms.

There was no deliberation, or even conversation. I knew, he knew, we knew. In fact, we'd already had this conversation, the one we didn't have in the moment we took in those two vertical bars on the blue-and-white test. We'd already been sad, we'd already thought through the impossible, the unreasonable, the undesirable, we'd already cried for this wish that wouldn't materialise in that moment. When I cried that day, it was for what I was preparing myself to go through. It was for what my body would endure, for my lost peace, for the betrayal, too. I didn't hesitate for a second because although I *did* want to have a child, this wasn't how I wanted it to happen, and in that precise instant, the rosy mental image I'd imagined for myself, of how a child *should* be welcomed into the world, was more important than anything else.

When it came time to make the choice, I didn't do it as an independent woman reclaiming control of her own life. I did it as a mother-to-be who didn't want her first child to arrive in less-than-ideal circumstances. I was no longer thinking of myself, but of the child I wanted to have one day, whom I already want to devote myself to. Bored to death reading about infant development, barely past the self-important stage of thinking that women who didn't even try to breastfeed didn't really want the best for their babies, I told myself: *I can't force a child to be born into a minuscule, poorly heated apartment, with no financial stability and no future prospects.* I imagined myself, eighteen years later, unable to pay for the education of this child, this little nothing that didn't even exist, and I winced. I wondered how the stress of a precarious pregnancy can impact a foetus that hadn't asked for any of this — I thought about cortisol levels, about the placenta, about the cigarettes I smoked when things weren't going well. None of it was possible. It wasn't what I'd imagined, this wasn't what I wanted, this wasn't how I dreamed of becoming a mother.

My dream as a person, as a woman, the life that I wanted for myself — it's only later that I would come to think of all of this.

Where did I get this strange idea that the future of a hypothetical child is more important than my own wellbeing?

For that, it's necessary to consider again this maternal desire that's difficult to fully understand. I was a responsible little girl. I took care of my stuffed animals and my books. I rocked my dolls, walked them in a miniature stroller; I loved pretending to be a shopkeeper or schoolteacher. I loved *taking care*. In doing so, I adopted all of the desired feminine attributes, and I wore them proudly. When my baby cousin was born, when I was nearly eleven years old, I wanted to be her godmother. I wanted that title like a reward: *Yes, we noticed that you were more mature than other children your age and that you would make a perfect little mother*. A year later, my baby brothers were born: surprise twins. Unintentionally, due to a mix of family upheaval, my mother's post-partum depression, and the gender-normative socialisation that I'd already adopted so eagerly, I found myself taking care of these babies in a manner that was completely inappropriate for a big sister who was herself still a child. I started developing my childcare skills very early. And I had a talent for it. Changing nappies, giving baths, comforting nighttime tears, feeding, picking up the dummy nonstop, trying to convince my young charges that the dummy was no longer needed, feeling a love so strong it overflowed: all that, I've known how to do for a long time.

When I was nearly a grown woman, it was no longer even a question for me. Of course I wanted to be a mother — what else would I want? There wasn't a lot I was certain about, so if that was taken from me ... At sixteen, I met the man who would hold my hand as my uterus emptied itself of its contents. I knew very quickly that I wanted to live my whole life with him, and in the language handed down from patriarchy, that takes the form of: 'I suddenly knew he would be the father of my children.' It was only a question of when. So no, before getting pregnant, I'd never doubted that I wanted children. Isn't that incredibly feminine? Shouldn't that be a red flag? I asked my lover when it was that he knew he wanted children. We talked about it fairly early on, when our relationship turned serious, but had he felt it, this wish, even before knowing that I existed?

When I decided to get an abortion, what I wanted — a child that I would think of before thinking of myself — wasn't actually what I wanted. It was the result of the complicated equation of being a woman, of having been raised as such, and of having fit the mould so comfortably. I had to have an abortion before I could reconceptualise a desire for motherhood that belonged entirely to me, where I wasn't shoved aside, a passenger in my own life, numb to my own future possibilities.

So, to celebrate making the decision official, and as reassurance that I wouldn't back out, I bought a pack of cigarettes, even though I rarely smoked. It was a cold, grey morning in October. A stiff wind was blowing, and my fingers, already turning blue, tightened around the tiny cup of coffee that I'd ordered at the corner bar where I'd bought the first of what would be a long series of cigarette packets. I needed them to keep going. Wrapped in my shapeless sweater, my hair in my eyes, I couldn't stop shaking. It took a thousand texts to my sister, my closest girlfriends, notes in my phone, and two cigarettes smoked like that on the sidewalk, staring at nothing, for me to absorb that this was happening to me.

When I called my doctor, I said, 'It's sort of urgent, I'm pregnant and I want an abortion.'

That set off a chain of events that I have never regretted. But as the process got underway, a gulf also widened within me, imperceptibly. I didn't know that having an abortion would be so hard for me. I didn't know what abortion could be.

WHERE ARE THE WOMEN
WHO'VE HAD ABORTIONS?

Abortion is invisible. It doesn't have a public presence. Once in a while, it appears in media coverage: the Polish no longer have access to it, the Argentinians finally have access to it. We talk about abortion in the public sphere only when it's a question of allowing or disallowing it. Then, statistics get trotted out, a few experts get to speak, a few women offer their first-hand experiences. During that media frenzy, there's a lot of noise, and we hear from just as many people who defend the right to free abortions without shame as we do from people who stigmatise women who have chosen to have abortions. It's not for feminists' lack of trying to bring this subject more to light, but it hasn't gained a foothold. Of course, there are exceptions that confirm the rule, cultural objects that raise the question, but if there's a generalisation to be made, it's this: abortion is invisible.

I'm a feminist, and I was interested in questions around sexual and reproductive health before I got pregnant. I was plugged into the right media, but I still had no idea of what a person went through during an abortion. I had the information, I had the political knowledge, but I didn't have access to first-hand stories or a way of identifying with them. Maybe it's because I write stories for a living, but I believe that the stories we tell are political, in both their content and their form.

In January 2019, Netflix released the first season of *Sex Education* (created by Laurie Nunn), which quickly won the hearts of viewers as well as critics. Its ageless teens, with their deliciously British accents, are as vibrant as they are touching, and the subjects addressed are done so with compassion. This show normalises. That's important. In Episode 3 ('Liftoff'), the teenage character Maeve has an abortion. I had never seen something like that, much less seen it handled like that. When I watched this episode — where a teen gets pregnant, never feels obligated to reveal the 'father' (there is no father because there is no child), and is accompanied to her abortion by a friend — I cried. I thought about everything that could have changed for me, if I had seen *Sex Education* years before when I was navigating becoming a sexually active person.

I thought, too, about the TV series and films that had, up to that point, provided everything I thought I knew about abortion. In *Juno* (directed by Jason Reitman and released in 2007), the discourse around abortion is very limited: if the character of Juno, pregnant at 16, opted to have an abortion, there would be no movie — an entirely different story would be told. In the scene that broaches abortion, Juno arrives at a clinic and is stopped outside by one of her classmates protesting abortion, who tells her: 'It has fingernails!' Several minutes later, after entering the depressing clinic, Juno turns around, sprints out, and the story begins.

In a podcast interview from 2019[ii] — shortly after Alabama passed what was then the strictest anti-abortion law in the country (outlawing abortion even in the case of rape or incest) and Georgia passed its 'heartbeat law', banning abortion after detection of a foetal heartbeat (around six weeks of pregnancy, before many women even know they're pregnant) — Diablo Cody, the screenwriter of *Juno*, said when asked about the film, 'I wasn't thinking as an activist. I wasn't thinking politically at all.' She added, 'I think I took the right to choose for granted at the time.'

It's interesting to note that many anti-abortion organisations praised *Juno* for its perceived 'pro-life'[2]

---

2   The American Catholic right that campaigns against abortion rights have helped themselves to the word 'life', dubbing themselves 'pro-life'. A pernicious semantic reversal, implying that the fight for free and accessible abortions is a fight 'against life', and therefore, through slippery association, 'pro-death'. In light of the number of women who die each year following illegal abortions, whom these conservatives don't give a crap about, it's understandable why this self-appointed label is a touchy subject. It's a cruel irony.

discourse, and that leaders of the American Catholic right personally reached out to thank the screenwriter for the film's stance on abortion. The film even inspired a conservative bill proposal in Ohio under the name 'Juno's bill'. It was a disaster for the writer, who was deeply pro-choice, but it's also very revealing, in my opinion, of the film's ambiguous message, in a political context where abortion is not always guaranteed. And where Diablo Cody perhaps erred by not adequately questioning the political reach of her work, my editors and I have spent long hours discussing a certain word, a certain turn of phrase, taking a thousand and one precautions in an attempt to prevent what happened to *Juno* from happening to this text.

Abortion can't be used as just another narrative device, introduced to advance the plot. Just as sexual violence or racism cannot be simple cogs in a story's machinery due to their serious, sensitive nature. It's important that they be treated with care and respect.

Juno came out in 2007 and at least made the effort to mention abortion as a possible choice. The final episodes of *Gilmore Girls*, on the other hand (a series created in 2000 by Amy Sherman-Palladino) came out in 2016. And in its nearly ten years on TV, this series that was so meaningful to so many women completely failed to mention abortion. In fact, the show never even says the word. And yet, multiple unplanned pregnancies happen in its 153 episodes. Lorelai's pregnancy is defended at all costs by her buttoned-up mother, Emily, and the only person who dares to think of 'getting rid of it' is Christopher's father, portrayed as your textbook curmudgeon. When Sookie gets pregnant again, even though she's only just emerging from two years of nappies and vomit, she's devastated. Lorelai, who's supposed to be her best friend, tells her, 'Sookie, you know you can't walk off a pregnancy, right?' Lane, Rory's best friend, gets pregnant after her first sexual encounter. It isn't happy news for her, either, with her rock 'n' roll dreams. But Rory's first reaction is to tell her, 'You're going to be a great mother!' Finally, in the series finale, filmed ten years after the first episode aired, we learn that Rory herself, now thirty years old, is pregnant. She doesn't know who the father is, but that's not what's important here: it's that the previous three episodes don't allow viewers to imagine that this is something that she wants. Here, still, the 'a-word' is never uttered. It's understandable that abortion was not a subject easily addressed when the original seven seasons aired: those years were marked by a significant taboo against abortion in US TV, and *Gilmore Girls* aired on a conservative network channel. But even so, it's difficult to extend a similar indulgence to the latest episodes produced for Netflix, created in a different political and cultural climate than the original series. It should have been even more crucial to bring up abortion in this new era because the new production company wouldn't have been such an obstacle, and because openly anti-abortion politics have once again returned to the US. But the creator of *Gilmore Girls* continued to use unplanned pregnancy as a plot device, without risking her own neck by treating the subject with the complexity that it deserves.[iii]

Obviously — and happily — things change, and television networks are no longer as hesitant to talk about abortion, and there are more and more interesting, true, and beautiful representations of this life experience that can happen to anyone who can get pregnant: *Sex Education*, which I mentioned previously, but also the film *Never Rarely Sometimes Always* (2020), the series *GLOW* (2019), and the film *Portrait of a Lady on Fire* (2019). In 2021, the film *Happening* (directed by Audrey Diwan) was released to high acclaim. This is an adaptation of the novel of the same title by Annie Ernaux, and it received the Golden Lion at the Venice Film Festival. In France, its release was notably accompanied by a project called 'Oui j'ai avorté' ('Yes, I had an abortion'), in the monthly women's political magazine *Causette*.[iv] Thirteen people spoke about their abortions. In the project's introduction, journalists Aurélia Blanc and Alizée Vincent emphasise, 'We had trouble finding women willing to speak on the record about this. Proof that the subject is still taboo.'

The fact that *Happening* was adapted for the big screen more than twenty years after its publication reveals something about the public debate around abortion. Was that amount of time necessary to show an illegal abortion on-screen, in all of its terrifying, harrowing realities — in much the same way that US TV series couldn't show abortion in the early 2000s? The dates line up. But is it also because it's time to reactivate our collective *memory* of abortion bans, because we're on the verge of forgetting what it *truly* is to no longer have access to legal abortion? In 2000, Annie Ernaux wrote:

> The fact that my personal experience of abortion, i.e. clandestinity, is a thing of the past does not seem a good enough reason to dismiss it. Paradoxically, when a new law abolishing discrimination is passed, former victims tend to remain silent on the grounds that 'now it's all over.' So what went on is surrounded by the same veil of secrecy as before.[v]

When I read these words, I was in Rouen, in Normandy (like she was in 1963), and I thought to myself, *They're still true, twenty-one years later*. The same veil of secrecy as before.

These new representations give me hope, though, that more and more people will have access to stories of abortion in addition to those presented in the mass media, when we're again — still — fighting for this right. I wholeheartedly believe that we need a multitude of stories to nourish our worldview, and, once we've encountered abortion on our own personal paths, to have multiple reference points to grab hold of.

It's not only from fiction that our perceptions are formed. I noticed when I decided to have an abortion that I didn't know anyone in my circles who'd done it before. Unsurprisingly, this was untrue: I didn't know anyone who *talked* about their abortion, which is markedly different. I'm not placing blame on women who have had painful experiences of abortion, or who prefer to keep these experiences private. As with any intimate life experience, I completely understand not wanting to talk someone's ear off about having had an abortion.

But still, I wonder why we hardly talk about it at all.

As I began my research for this book in 2020, I realised that I didn't have easy access to many accounts of abortion. In the past few years, after the collection of personal stories *J'ai avorté et je vais bien, merci* (I had an abortion, and I'm fine, thank you), edited by La Ville Brûle in 2012,[3] I discovered Aude Mermilliod's graphic novel *Il fallait que je vous le dise* (I had to tell you), as well as Sandra Vizzavona's account, *Interruption* (Termination). Reading these brought me face-to-face with a sense of purpose so similar to my own that it pierced me:

> My focus was not on the right to abortion, but
> on the right of those who've been through it to

---

3 This collection brings together the words of women whose abortions took place from before its legalisation in 1974 up to 2012. Unfortunately, it is no longer in print.

talk about it. The right to abortion has been inscribed in law for forty-five years, but its practice still must be done with discretion, if not in secrecy. The law allows us to have abortions, but society prevents us from talking about them. There are many of us who bow to this law of silence due to lingering embarrassment and guilt.[vi]

It seems that there are many of us, then, who feel the need for a certain amount of 'freedom of speech', a phrase that perhaps reflects the social progress of a century spent breaking down barriers. This similarity between approaches made me question, for a time, the necessity of my own story. Did the world really need another personal account of abortion?

I continued to read, to talk, and to listen, and I decided: yes. I decided that the stories of women are far from being so numerous that they should be whittled down, choosing between this one or that one. If white, cis-het men can retell the same story a hundred times, of an antihero going through a full-on mid-life crisis, without creating a marketplace bottleneck, then others can also seize their right to repeat, validate, hammer the message home.

It was during these hesitations that, in early spring 2021, I loaded myself into Juliette's car, and we left town together, picking up Claire on our way, heading to a retreat with maybe twenty other people to write and reflect on our writing. Space and time converged — in that confined space, the countryside racing past us — to create a mood that encouraged sharing: not a single cis man on the horizon, and four hours of asphalt swallowed by the wheels as we asked each other about our jobs and our projects. I got around to explaining this book that was taking root inside me, the different forms it had taken, and where it was headed in that moment. A snake-like book, a chameleon. Juliette and I talked about our abortions, and later in the weekend, Wendy and Aurélie would add their voices. Previously, I'd collected stories from Soriya, Laëtitia, and Carole. None of their stories were similar to mine, but they all resonated with me. We all shared a moment when things went sideways, when a decision we made left a slight jog in our timeline. In this company, I felt myself belonging. I realised, stupidly maybe, that for these stories to be shared, all we had to do was open our ears and our hearts. Walls and silence only persist when we allow them to. I believe, during the time that I was writing this book, that I assumed the role of ambassador, passing on information. A role that women are still so often refused, when we have so many things to say and share — a role we should seize for ourselves.

Abortion hides in the stories we leave untold, but also in those we share. Among ourselves, we pass on its ghost or its scar from generation to generation, in our evening murmurs, in our chats among friends.

THE UNTHINKABLE

Like many people who have abortions, I got pregnant while on birth control. In my circle, there were a few of us who got pregnant with an IUD — the rest of them all resulted in a baby, though I'm not aware of the reasons influencing those decisions. For many women, birth control means sexual activity, and when you're with the same partner for a certain amount of time, it's common to stop using the only contraception that protects against both pregnancy and STIs (condoms, that is, either internal or external) and instead turn to a method that is wholly under the woman's control.[4] Maybe it's because so

---

4   Aside from vasectomies (which are not always reversible), there are currently two methods of male birth control available in France. One involves biweekly testosterone injections, takes three months to be effective, and is not covered by the national

many of these IUD pregnancies happen where there are two parents present, who have already started their shared life together, that these pregnancies are continued, even if there had been no previous plans for a baby.

Personally, I very much identified with the words of the thinker bell hooks, writing here about the contraceptive pill in the 1970s:

> Responsible birth control liberated many women like myself who were pro-choice but not necessarily pro-abortion for ourselves from having to personally confront the issue.[vii]

Birth control, by preventing unplanned pregnancies as much as possible, put abortion in the category of subjects that I only thought about hypothetically, without considering it as something that could potentially happen to me. In one sense, I never wanted to have to think about it because no matter where I was on my maternal journey, abortion was a sensitive subject for me, personally. Even

---

health services. The other, commonly referred to as the 'thermal method', is not recognized by the WHO or the French minister of health, and is therefore considered unreliable. Put briefly: men don't have a lot to choose from. Furthermore, many women don't feel ready to trust their male partners to be responsible for birth control. We might wonder (with no ill-will) whether men have the necessary dedication to stay on top of a contraceptive treatment when the result of a mistake in birth control won't be embedded in their body. The debate is complex.

though I was convinced of the absolute necessity of free, accessible abortion for all, I didn't want to be a part of this 'all'. I didn't want to have to confront a choice that I knew on a subconscious level would not be easy for me.

An unplanned pregnancy while on birth control brings to light an uncomfortable, unthinkable idea. *If I was on birth control, it's because I didn't want to get pregnant.* There shouldn't have been even a moment of indecision. There was no doubt and no regret; I had my birth control as justification. I could say (to myself): 'Of course I don't want this, I *didn't* want this, and here's the proof.' And I thought that idea was all it would take for an abortion to be chosen, painless, and untroubled.

I thought it would be quick and easy, over and done.

When I shared this with the six women who were listening to my plans for this book, I realised how absurd my certainty had been. It was Élodie who responded in her slightly cracked, slightly veiled voice: 'It's incredible to imagine that something that affects the body like that wouldn't provoke something, like it never happened.' She said that there was denial there, of the link between the body and the mind, and I was struck by the truth of that.

After the initial euphoria of knowing that I could procreate, I felt an overwhelming anger toward my body, as if it were separate from myself, or more as if I were existing several steps removed from it, only engaging with my internal mechanics for a few medical check-ups. When I was anorexic in my teens, I wanted this body to disappear, for it to be thin enough to see through. Back then, I'd also thought that this confused desire to separate my mind from my body wouldn't affect my brain, the thoughts it produced, the ideas it formed. So I'd already made this mistake once before, and now, ten years later, I was making it again.

My abortion made me confront questions that I would have preferred not to, and made me confront my body, so uncontrollable in so many ways, but nevertheless intimately connected to my mind. The hormonal fluctuations, the mood swings, my changing silhouette, the bleeding, the vaginismus, are only some of the many symptoms that took root in my body, whose origin — my abortion that I chose, so painful in and of itself — was anchored in both my body and my mind.

When I talked with my girlfriends, who were also on birth control, about getting pregnant with my IUD, many of them told me that my misfortune terrified them. I don't doubt that; I hadn't wanted to consider it either: 'What if I have the bad luck of being part of the 0.1–0.6% of people whose birth control fails?' In the moment, though, I was more jaded than compassionate about their fear. *What do you want me to say, ladies? Yep, it happens, look me straight in the eyes when I tell you it happens, and not just to other people.* I told myself for a while that if I had asked myself that question, if I had really considered it, if I had *wanted to know*, maybe

I would have been a little more prepared and a little less afraid.

And I blamed myself, too, for assuming — and in so doing giving all others who, like myself, were affected by pregnancy — the burden of this responsibility. I wished I'd been able to protect myself from potential hurt.

During that time, my husband and everyone whose sperm is fertile 24/7 got to enjoy the comfort of not having to worry about all that, of never having to feel responsible for their partner's birth control failing and its consequences, even though without them none of this could happen. How are you supposed to feel personally concerned when you will never feel the consequences of this failure in your own body?

A PARTIAL AND SUBJECTIVE OVERVIEW OF ABORTION RIGHTS

My abortion was not complicated, technically speaking. A very early pregnancy, in a country where abortion is not only legal but also covered by national health services. I live in a large city where ob-gyn services are accessible — which is not the case everywhere in France, not even in every major city — and I had a strong support network. All of that, however, didn't prevent me from having a rough time during and after the experience. And of course, how can I not compare my situation to those, far more complicated, of women who don't have all the chances — all the privileges — that I had?

The more I document and the more I talk with other people who have had abortions, the more I realise to what extent abortion reinforces violence and silence. It's not my intention to create a theoretical or radical survey of abortion, and furthermore, I regularly have to remind myself of what I'm hoping to accomplish here, which is to tell my story. But because I'm a social animal, my own story is dotted with others I've come across in my journey.

For example, when reading *The Turnaway Study*, by researcher Diana Greene Foster, I discovered that in the United States, some states allow abortion up to viability of the foetus (twenty-two weeks). I was astonished. That's very late for a country where, in 2009, one of the few doctors performing abortions in the state of Kansas was killed by anti-abortion terrorists.[viii] Compare that to France, where abortion is banned country-wide after twelve weeks.[5] What's wrong with this picture? Foster recalls:

> Once, after I had given a talk at the University of
> California, Berkeley, about the Turnaway Study,
> a visiting scholar from Denmark approached me
> and shared what he thought was a clear solution
> to the mess that is abortion-rights politics in the
> United States. The Danes had already figured

5   In 2021, as a result of the Covid-19 health crisis, the legal limit for
     a medical abortion was extended from seven weeks of pregnancy
     to nine weeks. Despite a favorable opinion from the ethics
     committee, the proposition to extend the legal limit from twelve
     weeks of pregnancy to fourteen weeks was not passed.

this all out, he informed me, his tone growing exasperated. Why were Americans so backward? If people stopped advocating for access to later abortions and just agreed to set a nice low limit like Denmark's 12-week limit, which currently the vast majority of U.S. women seeking abortions would be able to meet, the controversy around abortion would evaporate.

She explains further on:

> Why might a first-trimester gestational limit work in Denmark? Because Denmark has the United Kingdom and the Netherlands nearby, where women can go when they are beyond 12 weeks. So Denmark gets its feel-good, we-have-it-all-figured-out solution, while the presence of English and Dutch services provides an escape valve that allows people seeking abortions beyond that limit to be served without upsetting the social contract.[ix]

I understand that if France, like Denmark, boasts about being a near-idyllic society when its abortion limits are much stricter than in the United States, it's because its stance on abortion is just as hypocritical as its stance on fertility treatments for all. To that point, there are many single women and lesbian couples who turn to fertility clinics in Belgium and Spain — even though this solution carries a cost premium, both financially and emotionally, and therefore is not accessible to all. And there are many women who, past the legal limits in France, travel to England or the Netherlands for their abortions.[x] Once again, this solution is not satisfactory because it excludes minors, financially disadvantaged or rural women, and undocumented women. It's worth bearing in mind that illegal abortions still happen in France for these marginalised groups, with all of the dangers that can entail.

Furthermore, it's important to remember that even though abortion was legalised in France in 1975, it has yet to be made easily accessible and normalised as healthcare. In the last fifteen years, 130 abortion clinics have closed, and dozens more are still under threat. The seven-day waiting period imposed upon people seeking abortions was done away with in 2015, but the 'double conscience clause'[6] continues to contribute to stigmatising abortion and those who turn to it for help.[xi] For years, the abortion rights group Planning Familial has been campaigning for family planning centres and midwives to be allowed to perform surgical abortions.

---

6   Every medical procedure in France is subject to a 'conscience clause', by which doctors have the right to refuse treatment or prescriptions based on personal, professional, or ethical convictions, and to refer patients to another doctor. But an additional conscience clause was added to abortion-specific legislation, influencing perceptions of abortion as 'abnormal' medical care, adding to its stigma.

In 2018, I hosted a conversation with the doctor and writer Martin Winckler for the book club that I co-led at the time. I learned, once again to my great surprise, that there is no legal limit for abortion in Canada: in theory, it's possible to terminate a pregnancy up until the eve of birth, with no need for justifications relying on foetal or maternal health. In practice, 87% of abortions in Canada are performed before twelve weeks of pregnancy, and only 1.1% are performed at twenty-one weeks or later.[xii]

I'm writing these words when, recently, the victories and defeats in the fight for free, accessible, safe abortions have continued to alternate in a sickening sequence. We'd hardly had a chance to celebrate the freedoms won by the Argentinians and Irish before we wept at those lost by the Polish and Texans. In 2021, the Texas government passed a law encouraging citizens to report anyone 'aiding and abetting' abortion (which can mean doctors and nurses, but also the taxi driver who provides a ride to an abortion clinic), with a bonus 'bounty' of $10,000 to those whose reports resulted in successful lawsuits.[xiii] Very quickly, a website was created allowing Texans to anonymously engage in this lucrative form of denunciation. As we've seen, this law is not the first attack on abortion rights in the United States, but it *is* the one that launched a wave of offensives that eventually saw the overturning, in 2022, of *Roe v. Wade*, the 1973 Supreme Court judgment that legalised abortion in the US.[xiv]

It's dizzying to follow the pernicious attacks against

abortion rights around the world, even in Europe, even in France where it feels like we're safe. Here, the 'Survivants' (Survivors) movement, led by a digital communications specialist, has developed online strategies over years with the explicit goal of manipulating young people into not considering abortion as a solution to unplanned pregnancy.[xv]

Elsewhere, the techniques vary, are adapted to other cultures and situations, and continue to weave a sticky web of taboo and shame to dissuade women from abortions.

TOO LATE

My abortion was on 19 October 2018. I don't forget dates easily. I remember the exact date of my first kiss, my first sexual encounter, so how could I forget the day of my abortion? Exactly ten days passed between my positive pregnancy test and the embryo ending up in the toilet bowl. About five weeks passed between the procreative act and the end of my pregnancy. It's so little. So little.

In the 'orthogenics' wing — the euphemistic name that they give to the place where abortions are performed and facilitated in hospitals in France — they gave me an informational brochure, but I already knew I wanted to have my abortion at home. Like other people who choose to have medical abortions at home, I needed to normalise the moment. I felt that if I spent the whole day at the hospital, if they stuck a machine in my body and sucked out my insides, it would leave a visible trace, like an inkblot on my calendar. My first appointment ended. I had to come back on Wednesday for a blood test, and the nurses would give me the pills and instructions for the abortion. We planned for me to expel the embryo on a Friday: my husband took the day off to be with me, and we thought the weekend would allow us enough time to get back to normal. I would need to come back in three weeks, to make sure that it had gone smoothly.

So it was just the two of us there for my abortion that October morning. I took the first pill very early and went back to sleep, his large hand dry against my stomach, which soon began twisting around itself. Several hours later, I took the second pill, and I didn't have long to wait before a violent cramp tore through me, and as I was walking down the stairs, I felt sliding out of my vagina, into my menstrual pad, a rush of blood and the embryo. It had the same consistency as a very large menstrual clot, but the colour was grey, like nothing I'd ever seen before. I knew then that it was over, and it had happened very fast, maybe even too fast. I continued to bleed for three more weeks, and it felt interminable, when it had all happened in only a few seconds.

I was very lucky: I was able to choose the abortion I wanted, I wasn't rushed by arbitrary limits or external pressures, like those women who learn of their pregnancies after France's twelve-week limit and have to travel to another country, or like those who find out about their pregnancies early, but are told to come back later in order to not have a medical abortion. From beginning to end, I had a choice.

I was also lucky to come into contact with relatively 'cool' health professionals. A compassionate doctor, nurses well-practised in abortions, nonjudgmental. True, there was that lab tech who, after consulting my chart when she was confirming the pregnancy through the blood test, said to me in a lightly accusatory tone: 'Wow, twenty-three years old, married, a baby ... you're not wasting any time!' I put her comment in perspective even as I ground my teeth: there was no way for her to know that I was terminating this pregnancy. And true, there was the ultrasound tech who confirmed the presence of an IUD alongside an embryo, and who thought it was a good idea to say to me with disdain: 'You need to have your IUD checked every year. If you don't, you can't complain if it's out of place.' Again, I put this in perspective: *Maybe she's right, maybe I didn't pay close enough attention*. Her suggestion followed me, throwing me into a storm of negative emotions.

Because five months earlier, I'd felt a bright pain in my abdomen, and true, I was afraid my IUD had moved. So I did what's recommended: I checked that the strings were there, feeling them with my fingertips right at the cervix, and then I went ahead and consulted my doctor. He explained that the position of the IUD didn't matter so much, and that as long as it was still there, it was doing its job. So I didn't worry beyond that: I told myself, as does every patient who trusts their doctor, that if he'd thought I needed an ultrasound to verify the situation, he would have ordered one.

I'd forgotten all about that until I caught the ultrasound tech's dark look, her wand still in my vagina. *I should have, maybe…* No. I did what I was supposed to. And while I hadn't checked my IUD every year — which I hadn't even been told to do by the doctor who'd done my insertion — how would that have prevented it from moving and no longer being effective, when there are potentially thirteen cycles, and therefore thirteen ovulations between placement checks? This is what I told myself, over and over, trying to smother the guilt that threatened to pull me under, trying to replace it with anger at that health professional and her vicious judgmental opinions.

It was only at my post-abortion check-up that the gynaecologist glanced at the image from that ultrasound (which, personally, I'd never once been tempted to look at) and reassured me, 'Your IUD was in the right place. And even if it had moved, that's not your fault.'

In fact, she was the only person during my abortion process who had kind words to offer about what I was going through. Words of reassurance. Which I needed. The general compassion and lack of judgment notwithstanding, I needed people to ask me how I was doing, and, after I asked for help, asking in what ways I wasn't doing well.

I've been writing this book for almost two years, and it's taken that length of time for me to realise that if I had the impression I was 'lucky' for having chanced upon 'cool' doctors, it's because I was expecting far worse. I knew there could have been someone who would have forced me to listen to the heartbeat, or watch the screen, who would have lied to me, or stopped me altogether. Who would have hurt me, or made me change my mind. I'd been telling myself that micro-judgments and light needling weren't a bad price to pay for access to an abortion. I'd been so well conditioned.

In *Ceci est notre post-partum* (This is our post-partum), Illana Weizman explains how society, including doctors and loved ones, abandons pregnant bodies once they cease to be pregnant. Bodies — and psyches, too. Reading about women who brought their pregnancies to term, I wondered what space we leave for the post-partum of abortion — without, of course, daring to use that expression, because 'post-gestum' bodies produced nothing, and what they expelled, they did so by choice. And yet we know that, physically, what happens during a medical abortion is that a miscarriage is triggered. So it would be logical to treat this body, if need be, as a wounded space that requires time to heal.

So sure, the number for a marriage counsellor was noted on my file in the family planning centre, and all

I had to do was pick up my phone and call. And I'll tell you: I didn't dare. I needed someone to *ask* me. I needed someone to suggest it. After emptying my uterus, after seeing that embryo in the toilet bowl and flushing away my rosy image of pregnancy, as my sanitary products remained soaked with blood two weeks on, and as my heart shattered with a nameless pain, I needed someone to ask me, *Are you all right?*

How are you feeling?

Is there anything you need help with?

Then maybe I would have cried sooner than I did, and no doubt I would have said that I felt sick to my stomach, that I was now terrified to let my partner penetrate me, and that I was afraid I'd destroyed the part of myself that had dreamt of being a mother someday.

I would have understood that I had the right to take the time I needed to reset.

During drinks with friends, I mentioned the announcement we'd received in the mail, and the effect it had had on me. Like a blender that had mixed up everything inside me. I put on a brave face and laughed it off, but I also wanted to share what had been on my mind — as happens when you feel safe in the company of people you trust. I've been told many times that I trust too easily. Apparently, it's important to be more selective about what to say and to whom, and if you aren't sure of how your confessions will be received, if you don't foresee hurtful words, it's because you are, deep down, a little stupid and not discreet enough. Personally, I'd like to live in a world where difficult experiences can be shared and welcomed, gently and respectfully. I'd like to live in a world where women can share our stories with each other — and not only under red tents[7] — and talk about the events that have rocked our foundations and widened our fault lines, without always being told that what takes place within our bodies is too dirty, too shameful to be shared.

So I shared: that it was difficult for me to receive that announcement, because the dates had blended in my head and made me painfully aware of my recently emptied belly. I grieved, on the verge of tears. My female friend looked at me tenderly, with compassion, my lover put his large, warm hand on my shoulder. My guy friend, though, not maliciously but not tactfully either, shrugged and said something along the lines of, 'Well, I mean, it's too late. It's not like you can put it back in.'

That's my aborted embryo he's talking about there.

---

7   Red tents refer to single-sex gatherings of women, often cisgender, who come to share experiences related to 'womanhood'. They are inspired by ancient traditions where menstruating people, considered to be 'impure', would spend time together for the duration of their periods, a chance to share a moment alone among women and share the important milestones of a woman's life (puberty, but also marriage pregnancy, menopause ...). Red tents have had a renaissance in Western culture beginning in the late 2010s, coinciding with the rise of attention paid to the 'sacred feminine'. We can criticise, of course, the essentialism of the 'sacred feminine' and the 'gatherings of women' where femininity comes back to genitalia, menstruations, and the ability to bear children.

I don't know what he was trying to tell me, but what I heard was that crying didn't help anything, that the past was past, and why dwell on it? I felt it like a slap, like a call to order. *Let's not talk about the uncomfortable reality that comes 'after'.* I was shocked by his harsh words, but that wasn't my only reaction. I think that what he said — indelicately, without sugar-coating — is what many people believe, even without realising it, about women who've recently had abortions.

I received compassion when I needed to fix the situation, I received sympathy for my unhappiness, my bad luck, really. *You poor thing, that's terrible, you must be so upset — but now that it's over, would you be so kind as to pipe down about it, please?*

But when is an abortion over, really?

We don't know what to do with all this grief, but I believe women don't need people to propose solutions for them, or try to save them. They simply need spaces to lay down their griefs and their doubts, if they have them.

The entire time that I was healing from my chosen-yet-painful abortion, I avoided comparing my experience to that of pregnancy or motherhood. It felt indecent to me, for reasons I couldn't fully explain to myself — maybe because I'm still ignorant of the realities of motherhood, of what it inscribes in body and life. But several years after the fact, the parallels come back to me in the conversations that I have with people who are now mothers, who had abortions previously.

They tell me that since abortion is a choice, society wants it to be a choice that is easy and untroubled. I think, ferociously, my agreement reinforced by the range of emotions visible in their eyes, that those who have had abortions are generally told: *You've made your bed, so lie in it*. You wanted it, you got it, now shut your mouth and smile. And I ask these women if that isn't unlike what those who become mothers are also told: *You wanted it, you got it, now shut your mouth and smile*. Don't mention the difficulties that you're going through because it's not done, it's unseemly, it's immoral, it's unattractive. You're happy you had a child. You're happy you had an abortion. It's all white, because if it were black or even a little grey, it would be too complicated.

Women don't have the right to be complex. Our multiple dimensions don't have the luxury of unfolding, so narrow is the space we're afforded.

SELFISHNESSES

I like to think I'm a good person. I'm afraid of appearing selfish, and sometimes that prevents me from making decisions that are beneficial to me because I don't want to disappoint people or have them think I put myself first. But of course, I put these fears to the test when I decided to have an abortion. What's more selfish than that? Besides having a child, of course. So, we're all in the same boat, women with uteruses empty and full, making our acrobatic justifications; some of them are reasonable, and others we cling to like boulders in a current. Too often we mistake selfishness for malicious intent — especially when the subject proposing this selfishness is feminine, because women don't have the right to be their own priority.

During my own self-reflections, I felt like I could find as many good reasons to have an abortion as to not, and it was at that moment that I became aware of a very simple fact that should suffice in and of itself: There are no good reasons, or bad ones, other than those that we feel deeply in our marrow. Those that never leave us, those that occupy our every thought and, in the end, make the decision obvious.

If we don't collectively accept that the reasons for an abortion are infinitely numerous and infinitely unique, then we cannot discuss abortion with any semblance of calm. The limits of the debate need to be clearly on the table: what's true for me is true only for me, and everything true for me is, by default, correct and legitimate.

When it comes to bodies and experiences, it's not the number that strengthens the argument. It's tempting to present the right to abortion in its best light. Like me, with my cut-and-dried story of getting pregnant while on birth control, or like the rhetoric that places the emphasis on pregnancies resulting from rape or incest. The truth is that anyone should be able to have an abortion without shame, even when it's because you weren't paying close enough attention, even when you were irresponsible, even when you fuck up. Having a child should never be a punishment.

To be able to talk about abortion together properly, we need to feel, deep down, that it's a subject not up for negotiation — and therefore feel that we have a shared safe space to grow alongside others that we meet along our way, to speak our truths without having them questioned.

The selfishness most often pointed out when challenging abortion (aside from taking away the possible life of a potential human being) is that the right to fatherhood is taken away from the progenitor, who donated half the DNA beginning to replicate itself in a womb that isn't his. In feminist spaces, the stance is firm. They chant at protests, bellowing: 'No uterus, no opinion!' They point out, rightly, the old men who legislate our bodies without ever going through the emotions or difficulties inherent to an unplanned pregnancy. They can sense, shuddering, that if men are allowed to talk about abortion, the existing gulf will widen, and men will gain even more traction to attack our right to govern our own bodies.

I hesitate to talk about men's place in abortion. But I feel that in refraining from discussing it out of fear of seeing my arguments appropriated by the bad faith camp with a stranglehold on the conversation, I'm contributing to lost opportunities to deepen these conversations. And I no longer know if that's helping us at all.

Because, to be honest, I don't know if I would have had an abortion if my husband hadn't been 100% behind me. If he'd hesitated, if he'd started tweaking our finances to make a family of three viable, if he'd projected himself into the near future with a baby that both of us wanted together, then maybe I wouldn't have been so determined. And inversely, we'd already had this conversation when I was eighteen, and my period was late by eight days. While

I, living with one foot in a fantasy world and already in a relationship with the man of my life, could envision myself becoming a mother at that moment (whether that would have been a good idea or not isn't the question here), it was his total rejection of that level of responsibility so early in his life that most definitely tipped the scales. Yes, it's politically delicate, but I would be lying if I said without hesitation that I made my decision alone and that nothing could have changed my mind.

When it comes down to it: when we exclude men from the abortion conversation, isn't that also continuing to protect them and free them from all responsibility? Over and over, we're told that it takes two people of opposite sex to risk a pregnancy. It's said with regard to shouldering the responsibility for birth control, and it should continue to be said when the unplanned happens.

If a woman makes her decision without consulting the man she had sexual relations with, that's her right, and it should be inalienable. But that is not to be confused with the systematic exclusion of men, as if in the end it's not about women's right to choose without external pressures, but about men's right to not be bothered by the consequences of their coital ejaculations. I worry that in always removing men from the results of birth-control failures (or in the numerous instances when they insist on not wearing a condom, when they don't offer to pay for half of non-reimbursed contraception, or when they don't see sex as anything other than vaginal penetration for their own benefit), they continue to be sheltered from the very concrete outcomes of their ejaculations.

By leaving space for my husband in my abortion, I also left space for his emotions. It is frequently and rightly lamented that men don't use a palette of emotions large enough to unpack the ordeals they go through. I'm personally convinced that this vocabulary, lacking because either it wasn't taught in childhood or it was stamped out, is part of the problem of masculinity, one of the bedrocks of patriarchy.

My husband was affected by my pregnancy and by the abortion that we experienced together. Even though I'm the one who bore the physical consequences, he has the right to be impacted by it. We both found it important to talk about it with each other, to share our experiences, to enrich our vocabulary, as well as to speak about it separately, each with our own mental health professionals, to sift through our thoughts to be able to heal, individually and as a couple.

I'm not suggesting that men have the right to influence their pregnant partner's decision regardless of the nature of their relationship. It's because I was pregnant with the man that I love, who respects me and whom I want to raise a child with someday, that I can't imagine deciding to have an abortion without taking his opinion into account. In plenty of situations, the progenitor's opinion doesn't have to matter. In plenty of others, it can carry weight, as with women who want a child and who terminate a pregnancy even when they're in a happy heterosexual relationship — there must be more of us, I can't be the only one.

The idea occurred to me that if we (feminists) have so much trouble making room for men who might want to discuss abortion, it's because we're hyper-aware of the fact that women still don't have the right to talk about it freely. It's those constantly exasperating double standards that always fall in favour of men — who have the right to say everything, think everything — that makes their comments on such a sensitive topic so bitter to us. Comments that smother women's by default, because we still live in a society where the voices of women have no value, where a thousand, a hundred thousand, stories from women can be invalidated by one opposing comment from a man.

So we stand today at a tipping point. Perhaps it's not yet the moment to include men in this conversation, but do we really want to exclude them forever? I believe in the political and therapeutic force of reserving certain gatherings for women. However, I also believe that such gatherings are a fundamental and necessary part, but not an end in themselves, of raising and discussing important issues at stake in creating the society we want.

Here, the question of the legitimacy of men's opinions in abortion legislation (there is none; in this case the principal of 'no uterus, no opinion' is essential) should be distinct from the space given to the experiences of men who accompany women during their abortions. That very much means that men who don't accompany women, to my mind, still don't get a say. But I have trouble imagining a new reality, freer and happier, where men still wouldn't have the right to verbalise and to process the emotions that they face.

While we await this new reality, the injunctions imposed upon people who have abortions (or wish to have abortions) continue to loom like a blade waiting to fall. The expectation that women should be generous (including offering the ultimate gift of life) no matter the cost to themselves, to me is one of the most absurd.

We're supposed to feel guilty about snuffing out life in the egg. How selfish is that? I admit that this way of thinking didn't even cross my mind when I made my decision. I thought then that abortion was a stopover in my life as a person who wanted to be a mother. As I said previously: in a certain way, it was in thinking about the existence this child would have had, if it had been born into those conditions, that I realised this wasn't what I wanted to offer it. I don't feel selfish for refusing to drop a minuscule human being into this furious world without being able to offer it better. It seems to me that this is as worthy a reason for women who want to be mothers one day (but not at a certain unideal moment), as for women who have no intention at all of being mothers, ever. When the anti-abortion activists want children to be born no matter the circumstances that will welcome them — economic as well as emotional — who are they helping? The children? As a society, wouldn't it be preferable if all children were born into the best environment possible to face life? Are those advocating against abortion also advocating for a society that's more egalitarian, less harsh, for life to be easier for all?

Here I want to talk about reproductive justice. This fight for social justice isn't just the fight for abortion rights. It's also a fight for parents to be able to care for their children for as long as necessary, for everyone who wants to have children to have them, and in the best conditions possible. Isn't that an ambitious and joyful social project?

It was when I started working to understand why I wasn't processing my abortion, why my body and mind hadn't recovered from it quickly and easily, that I deconstructed, brick by brick, with determination, the selfishness I felt of having chosen myself over what was growing within me.

If ... if if if. I could wonder about the ifs and ands all day, but it's not far-fetched to think that if I hadn't chosen abortion, then I wouldn't have had the opportunity, the energy, the means, to write until the small hours of the morning, for no money (or almost), until finally publishing my first book. If I'd been pre-occupied with putting a child into the world and taking care of it during the summer of 2019, I surely wouldn't have continued to advocate, I wouldn't have written the blog piece that caught the attention of my editors, I wouldn't have written my book, I wouldn't have improved my financial stability.

After my abortion, I was filled with rage at not having been in a situation that would have allowed me to see that pregnancy through. I imagined another life for myself where I had a comfortable salary in a job where I worked thirty-five hours a week. Since it's statistically impossible to earn a living from writing at twenty-three years old, that parallel dimension also entailed that writing would no longer be at the centre of my existence. That could have been a great existence, but it wasn't the one that I aspired to, and deeply.

Choosing my abortion gave me the space to realise myself.

There was a window, between when I stopped bleeding and when I began writing this text, where I ended up questioning whether I wanted to be a mother. I was no longer sure that it was compatible with my new plans. It all started with a sentence from Jeanette Winterson:

> I can't find a model, a female literary model who did the work she wanted to do and led an ordinary heterosexual life and had children. Where is she?[xvi]

Fear ran up my spine, launching me into a productive panic. I read articles that shed light on the role of birth control in the lives of great writers such as Angela Davis and Doris Lessing.[xvii] As I let writing take a greater place in my life, I began to identify more and more with these creative women, these feminine creatives, whose greatest work on the earth was *not* bearing and raising children. I remembered the dedication in Gloria Steinem's autobiography, *My Life on the Road*:

> This book is dedicated to: Dr. John Sharpe of London, who in 1957, a decade before physicians in England could legally perform an abortion for any reason other than the health of the woman, took the considerable risk of referring for an abortion a twenty-two-year-old American on her way to India. [...]

> [H]e said, 'You must promise me two things. First, you will not tell anyone my name. Second, you will do what you want to do with your life. [...]

> I've done the best I could with my life.[xviii]

I became aware of what, about motherhood, had prevented women in the past from conserving their artistic identity, as well as what could swallow me as well if I wasn't careful, and would have obliterated me if I'd had a child before having the time to reflect on my dreams, what I hope to be and accomplish. I very much wished to do what I wanted with my life, I was terrified of losing myself along the way, and I told myself that I would rather *not* be a mother if that meant I *could* be a writer. When I chose my abortion, I was also making this choice.

I met some of the women Jeanette Winterson couldn't find. I know that they exist, and I hold them close to my heart: they inspire me. What they have in common is that, when creating their families, they all questioned the heteropatriarchal family model. Now, what had seemed a contradiction to me no longer is. Concretely, inequalities within heterosexual couples (in addition to other forms of social inequalities) mean that a lot of new mothers are swallowed by motherhood, to the point that they struggle to explore other facets of themselves for an unspecified amount of time. But I want, need, to believe that this is not inevitable. That this is not the natural order of things.

SHAME

For a long time, I assumed Annie Ernaux's book *Shame* was the one about her abortion.[8] It was only in trawling through her list of works, all titled so simply, that I realised my mistake. It was yet another moment that revealed my own subconscious discomfort around the topic of abortion. I called myself a feminist, and said that I'd never doubted the importance of free, accessible abortion *without stigma*, and that's true ... until I had to consider abortion as a personal matter. In relation to my own body. Because surely it could never happen to me — I'd done

---

8   *La honte* was published in 1997 by Gallimard (published as *Shame* in English translation in 1998 by Seven Stories Press) and is the story of Annie Ernaux's family upbringing, in which she was caught between her religious education in rural France, and her desire to see more, 'better' parts of the world.

everything right. I hadn't yet woken up to the fact that shame was deeply engrained within me, and that I would suffer from it despite my best intentions.

I waited a year and a half before telling my mother about my abortion. Without this book on the horizon, about to be visible and out in the world, and which I would be proud of, maybe I never would have broken that silence. (I tend to save the more hidden parts of my life for my writing, in hopes that the words will bridge what my voice cannot.) Part of me very much wants to brush off my abortion as an inconsequential bump in the road. When I confide something like this to my mother, though, it's impossible to deny the gravity of it. I don't tell her everything, but what I do tell her is sincere and true.

So when she had to come with me to an important doctor's appointment where my medical history would be discussed, the referral notes from my doctor included these simple words: *pregnancy with IUD — terminated.* The secret was going to be aired, one way or another. A little before setting out for the hospital, sitting and knitting with her, the activity that brings us together, I braced myself and I confessed.

A confession, like a crime.

I was so embarrassed for having put myself in the predicament of needing an abortion. What a stain on my record. Not that my mother would ever have made me feel that way. That was all me, my own mind's projection, but the fact that that's what I was projecting showed I wasn't in the best frame of mind.

I got married very young. That fact never fails to astonish people: feminist, radical, anarchist, but married, to a cisgender man, at twenty?

Several years ago, I went back to school and I met a lot of new people all at once, one of whom said to me: 'Isn't it mostly welfare chicks that get married young, then pop out a ton of kids?'

I'm not so sure about the accuracy of that off-the-cuff population study, but it's undeniable that these days, getting married young suggests the plot of an old made-for-TV movie from the US. They were prom king and queen, she got pregnant the summer after graduation, they had to get married, and now he works in insurance, a long way from his dream of being an NFL quarterback. Having children 'early' (let's say before twenty-five) seems, in the eyes of the social class that decides the laws of good taste, more like a failure than an enlightened choice.

Getting pregnant very (or too) young is humiliating. It's shameful. Unplanned pregnancy throws a harsh light on the sexuality of the young woman affected. *Look. You had sex? What did you think would happen, you impertinent chit? You'd better not be thinking of having control over your body after that.*

To speak is to bring into existence. On the individual level, it's important for shaping yourself, defining yourself, and being connected with others. At the political level, it's essential for increasing visibility and normalising. Shame, though, has an ugly, useless power: making people with lived experience keep it to themselves. We don't talk about things we're ashamed of; we don't open up about things that make us want to go into hiding, to disappear, to be someone else. I waited ten years to talk to a shrink about my bisexuality, because I was ashamed (first for not being straight, then for not being queer enough — will we ever get off this nausea-inducing merry-go-round?), like I waited a year and a half to talk to my mother about my abortion. Shame keeps tabs on us and exerts social control; there is no shame without society, without its judgmental looks, without its norms to deviate from, to make us understand that we *should* feel ashamed.

So at first that's what I did. Accidentally getting pregnant, in the twenty-first century, with the medical awareness and education that I'd received, wasn't very dignified of me. I was ashamed not to live up to the expectations my social class had instilled in me, as if total bodily control came in the same hospital bag as piano lessons and private school. My complaint of 'I did everything I was supposed to, this is just bad luck' throws under the bus everyone who might not have done *everything they were supposed to*, whatever that means. At its core, that mindset implied that if I were blameless, other women could still be blamed for their own situations. And that I was better than them: the airheads, the flakes, the reckless risk-takers. But at my lowest point, it was a relief to follow this line of thought to lighten the shame of my so-called respectable abortion circumstances. A despicable feeling of superiority, evidence of a nearly unconscious classist contempt.

There is no shame private enough that the hurled judgments don't splatter others on impact. We try to untangle ourselves from it, but sometimes it sticks to the skin like nasty plastic wrap.

In July 2021, Emmanuel Macron did an interview with *ELLE* magazine. When asked his thoughts on parliament's rejection of the proposed law aiming to raise the legal limit of abortion from fourteen to sixteen weeks, he said:

> I'm not in favour of it. [...] I've taken into
> consideration the trauma for a woman having
> an abortion [...] with much respect to those who
> think it's not a problem to have an abortion at
> sixteen weeks. All gynaecologists say that it's
> more traumatising at that point.

Then, the final insult:

> I respect [the conscience clause]. We must [...]
> renew our approach to this fight [abortion] from
> all angles, notably by offering guidance much

earlier to young girls and young women who receive no support in certain neighbourhoods.[xix]

This response from the French president is filled with lies and errors.

As for the overall trauma inflicted by abortion, as for the trauma of having an abortion at sixteen weeks compared to fourteen, studies like The Turnaway Study prove that these statements rely on no solid data and contradict observed reality. As for the statement 'all gynaecologists say', one might notably look to the community of feminist health practitioners 'Pour une MEUF' to understand that a subset of doctors does disagree with this dogmatic discourse.[xx] Finally, speaking only of 'young girls and young women' encourages the idea that all women who have abortions are young, which is not the case.[xxi] But most of all, I find it interesting that his response relies so specifically on the sensitive assumption of shame.

Speaking from his position about trauma and the pseudo-consensus of professionals, Macron informs women who are not traumatised by their abortions that they are not normal. In not questioning the conscience clause, the president classifies abortion as a subject open for debate, one on which opinions are allowed to diverge, so some can see it as immoral or not.[9] And finally, in emphasising

---

9   We could in fact consider abortion instead as a patient's right to enjoy her body as she sees fit, and to seek treatment for it as necessary.

'certain neighbourhoods',[10] he's feeding the classist idea that women from lower classes have a higher risk of unintentional pregnancy.[11]

If even the president goes down that path, it illustrates how heavy the burden of shame is, and how hard it is to be rid of it.

I'm at the kitchen table with my shame and my tea, wrapped in a blanket, and it's only now that I'm beginning to understand that my own feelings of shame never meant that I was guilty. There's nothing to atone for, I was never at fault — and neither are any of the other people who choose abortion. This censure around abortion is only there to serve the interests of patriarchy. It's always women who have to shut their mouths. It's always the oppressed who have to hold their tongues. They hold us on a leash, they muzzle us, because the second our voices ring out at full volume, it will become completely undeniable that society is not functioning, not at the same speed for everyone, and that is intolerable.

---

10 In politician-speak, that amounts to saying 'poor neighbourhoods' without admitting it, because that would be an admission that there are poor people in France and that we let them die.

11 And yet, if women from the lower classes outnumber those from more comfortable classes in seeking abortions, this doesn't mean that they have a higher risk of unwanted pregnancy. The only thing that this statistic tells us is that they are aware of the difficulties of raising a child in unfavourable economic conditions. This proves nothing except that women who have abortions do so in full awareness of the factors at play.

GRIEF

I'm once again visiting friends at their home, where I'd holed up several weeks after my abortion. Incidentally, it's also here that, nine months ago now, I made the decision to go off the pill, with the intention of getting pregnant. I'm here, and I'm waiting for my period, which isn't coming. Confusingly, I have the impression that the story that I'm trying to tell, the story being written as I live it, will not be able to come to a close without this rather puerile happy end. I want to shout at the sky: *Okay, I'm ready, let's wrap this story up.*

Ever since this text began to germinate inside me, my life changed so much that I had to start over fresh several times to find the right track — I'm not necessarily more confident having taken this route, where my setbacks in writing echo my setbacks in life, but that seems to me more logical and feasible than pretending that I'm unchanged. My relationship with my abortion over two-and-a-half years has evolved, and recounting it is an important part of the process.

My abortion left me completely exhausted.

This feeling is not necessarily shared by all who have abortions, but I was affected by the experience, profoundly changed. My abortion forced me to look at myself, as I truly was, naked and vulnerable. I'm beginning to wonder if, maybe, it was my abortion that made me an adult.

No, I didn't have a pleasant abortion experience. For a long time, I retained the image of the greyish embryo between my legs, and the memory of feeling it detach from my body. From that brief time of being pregnant, I retained a body already altered, a bra one size up that I hadn't got rid of. I had to learn to be confident, not in my body that never has been a separate entity from my conscience, but in my capacity to navigate the ruts that inevitably appear on the road of existence.

I took such a long time to grieve.

But first, I should clarify: grieve? For what, if I didn't want a child at that time, and if I didn't regret it?

I smile as I retrace my steps in my digital planner. I unravel another memory, in another dimension. Three days before my abortion, I was waiting in an aseptic room before one of my last job interviews. Director of communications at the university library — that would have made for an impressive line on my CV. I was trying to focus on the future that was about to take place. But now several years later, my head above water, having found my place in the universe, I can say it. That in that moment, I already felt that what was afoot inside me was more important than what I was going to try to prove to a panel of strangers who weren't going to hire me. The interview ended up being a minor disaster, but I walked out of it almost giddy. It was my right to fail a job interview; I was pregnant, the hell with it.

Scrolling in my phone where I religiously record my life (the FAANGs love me), I noticed that, quite the opposite of what I'd felt in the moment, my life hadn't stopped after my abortion. Even when I was still bleeding profusely, I had more interviews (none successful), saw friends, polished the novel that I would publish three years later. I saw movies, I went out to eat, I visited my grandparents. It was only internally that the machinery needed time to reset.

I had never experienced grief. The people close to me who had died in my lifetime were closer to others than to me. I didn't know what it was to lose what I'd taken for granted.

My carefree attitude, the comfortable illusion that I was in control of my own destiny, captain of my soul ... the abortion turned all that on its head. I reconsidered everything, relearned everything, starting with who I was. I thought my path would be straight and smooth, but here I was faced with roller coasters that were forcing me to consider reality: the path had never been straight or smooth, because life is never a long, quiet river. So I imagine that, in a way, my longest, most painful grief was for who I'd thought I was, as the sum of my parts. A young woman who clearly checked 'o pregnancy o child' on her blood-donation forms. The woman who arrogantly thought that abortion would never be a question she would have to personally confront — and when that turned out to be false, was convinced that it wouldn't affect her in the slightest, because she was above all that.

For a few months I've been searching for the well of emotions that formed in the wake of those October days, already so long ago. I can't access it anymore; in my mind it's covered, capped, almost condemned. But perhaps in this newly established distance, the mourning process has been continuing slowly, healing tissues unnoticed.

I have to say, that date will probably never leave me. In the darkness of my first concert post-pandemic, it occurred to me that the last time I'd seen a live show, I'd had an embryo in my belly. I cried. Dates leave a mark upon me, mile markers on the road, proof that I've survived, after thinking myself weak for so long. But just because I'll never forget my abortion doesn't mean I haven't moved forward. I want to say that I'm not traumatised by my abortion — it's always front of mind because it was a defining moment for me. I needed time to detach myself from it, not because it was horrible and sordid, but because I'm a person for whom an incident like that will have a deep impact, will cause a tectonic shift, will resurface old, forgotten questions for reconsideration.

I want to say, too, that there needs to be — we need to *create* — spaces where feelings of ambiguity, negativity, sadness, and insecurity can be shared and received, in company, out in the open. The experience of abortion is just one experience among many made more difficult by loneliness. Connection is a particle accelerator of serenity.

Today, while I wait for my period, hoping it doesn't come, I feel a peace that's still recent. It's still new within me, the certainty that I had to grow beyond what happened. Still new, the certainty that I will heal from it.

HEALING

Real life isn't a fairytale. I'm writing the end of this book while bleeding heavily, my lower belly twisted in painful cramps, tired from PMS that's lasted too long. But it's nice out, the coffee is good, and life goes on.

While reading *The Turnaway Study*, I held onto this sentence in particular:

> [A]bortion can be a normal part of planning a family and living a meaningful life.[xxii]

I read that and clung to it. I was lucky to be part of a community that was strong and resilient, and even if I still felt a little tender and sensitive, I was getting through it. This simple sentence gave me momentum: abortion can be normal. It's not the end of the world; quite the opposite, it can be the beginning. A voice murmured inside me: *You'll see, you'll pick yourself back up from this.*[12]

After examining this subject from every angle, I have to conclude that in the end I needed only a few simple ingredients to overcome my grief: time, love, and words.

The ever-flowing time that delivers the promise of new sprouts to a barren landscape is the same time that brings clarity. Sometimes it takes long months, maybe years, of distance to look back and understand the full meaning of a split-second decision that has never once been anything but the right one. Time is needed to rest after an event that overwhelms, at least a little, both the body and the mind. Love has been proven: women have better abortion experiences when they have a caring support network that doesn't judge their choice. And words are necessary, too, it's obvious. This gets at the heart of the personal and political. If every woman keeps quiet about her abortion(s), maybe it's not due to restraint as much as it is to shame — but if we say the word and share the experience, more tongues will loosen and more

---

12 Between finishing the draft and the edits for this book (books take so long to make ...), I got pregnant. I made the last edits through a fog of fatigue that was like an old friend I'd had a falling out with. During the long months between my decision to go off birth control and the (once again) positive pregnancy test, I often thought, despite my best efforts: 'What if I wasted my only chance?' I didn't know what to do about that thought except to take tender care of it, alongside everything else I was struggling to process.

stories will flow, an inexorable rising tide that will crash against every barrier.

I believe that time, love, and words are the foundations of a *community*, referring to all the little societies that contribute to forming the larger one, a safe space where we can evolve safely. The wider world will always be more difficult, more cruel, and less welcoming than the families of our own creation. That's why communities are important — to give us the tools, the rest, and the care to arm ourselves to better take on the world.

What communities can we build to encourage positive abortions? My conversations with other people who have had abortions form the beginnings of an answer.

Soriya told me, over a burger at our first real-life meet-up, about how talking openly about her abortion, publicly and bluntly, cost her the support (already fragile and conditional) of her family. She told me that the problem for them wasn't the accidental pregnancy. No, the problem was her talking about it, without even having the decency of feeling the shame she was expected to.

Carole told me about the abortion that tore her apart. She loved the idea of being a mother — but it was her circumstances that drove her to make the choice, and though she didn't regret it, she also wasn't processing it. And that's a difficult thing to declare openly, because in the twenty-first century, we're pressured to be proud of every right we've won, even if it turns our stomachs.

Anouchka receives a bouquet of flowers from her best

friend on the anniversary of her abortion. She promised me, when I told her about my sadness at being alone on that date my belly remembers so clearly, that she would think of me the next 19 October. And she kept her promise.

In the waiting room at an abortion clinic in the US, patients write in a journal that they leave for those who come later: Martina felt less alone, reading the stories of women who came before her, who shared similar situations, all nevertheless unique in their own ways.[xxiii]

Cléa is a doula. She speaks about perinatal grief and includes abortion in that scope. She proposes doing a ceremony with me to bid farewell to my terminated pregnancy, to that branch in my timeline that I edited out. And Wendy maintains a similar ritual, years after her abortion. It's what she needed.

After my conversation with Juliette in the car, after months of writing, I realised that I aspire to a society that is less solitary, in which births, miscarriages, abortions, but also sicknesses and deaths, are cared for collectively. I'm no longer afraid of appearing improper, quite the opposite — I want hardships to be shared as much as joys, and for the struggles our bodies go through not to be further burdened by secrecy. If I could go back in time, I would choose to have my abortion in the presence of my sister and friends; I would surround myself with sisterhood in that moment of extreme vulnerability. I would put this page of my life into the hands of the collective, for the story to be written in broad daylight. While we wait for men to do the work, finally, of finding their way toward their humanity, their full palette of emotions, it looks like we can only count on ourselves, women and gender minorities, to imagine these spaces where vulnerability is not a thing of shame.

I think I finally understand, at the tail end of the journey of writing this book, why the phrase 'I had an abortion, and I'm fine, thanks' was, is, and will continue to be significant. It proclaims: look, I'm alive, I'm a whole, complete person. My abortion is not my identity, I have other things to offer to the world and other things to do with my existence. My abortion is not the scar that defines me.

But while it's necessary to talk about it in order to be heard, I don't mind doing so. It's not my defining scar, and I do have other things to offer, but I *also* have this to offer, and *also* this story to tell. I thought abortion would need to become a neutral topic before one could speak calmly about real, ambiguous, unpleasant experiences related to it. I told myself that as long as there are agendas and victories and defeats, talking about it honestly would be disastrous. Abortion continues to be a delicate open political wound. We're afraid it will get infected, so we avoid it carefully. Maybe we should be addressing the problem from the other direction: maybe it's in talking about our experiences, every personal, private detail, that the subject will be neutralised. That we'll create non-polarised spaces. We have to rise above the all-out brawl over our rights to invent a new conversation.

Months ago, my husband and I were cooking a leisurely meal and talking about the abortion, the traces it left on us and between us. He said: 'Maybe it will never really be healed for us until we have that child we wanted, that we could have now.' I had to mull that over.

There's truth in that. Not so much in that a living child could replace the ghost of another that was never born. No, more that the injuries in need of healing within me fall into three categories. First, I have to rediscover a connection with my body, my entire person, no longer trying to separate the physical from the mental as soon as one or the other escapes from the illusion of my control. Then, there are the questions that are deeply personal — like, what I expect of motherhood, about my life and who I am, a philosophical chasm as uncomfortable as it is fascinating to explore. Finally, there's everything related to material necessities, falling outside the limits of personal control. My anger and rage have cooled now that I'm no longer poor and afraid that my meagre comforts in life will be swept away — as it happens, it's only now that these circumstances have changed that I can calmly entertain the idea of a planned pregnancy. But I'm not forgetting that, separate from my personal aspirations, it was my economic situation that steered me toward abortion. I don't forget that I'm advocating for a society where everyone would have the means to make these life decisions without worrying first about their bank account.

And it's in this regard that abortion will always be political. The ways in which we experience it and its long-term impacts (or lack thereof) are directly correlated to the society we live in. There will probably always be people who have unplanned pregnancies and who want to terminate them. Abortion is not the problem, just like taking paracetamol for a headache is not the problem: abortion is the solution, medically safe and indispensable. The problem is the obstacles placed to impede women who just want to live their lives, the best they can.

ACKNOWLEDGEMENTS

This account was the most difficult I've ever written in my life — and sure, I'm young, but still. I wouldn't have managed it without the support of those people who listened to my doubts, who gave me advice, who reassured and supported me, as well as those who shared parts of their own journeys as I was writing this text:

Fauve, Soriya, Laëtitia, Carole, Juliette, Wendy, Aurélie, Marcia, Élodie, Claire, Anaïs, Sabrina, Léane.

Special thanks to:

Julie Finidori, my agent and friend, for her solid, reassuring presence through all of the beautiful adventures that now punctuate my life,

Coline Charpentier and Juliette Dimet, my editors, for their faith in this project from the very beginning of our respective paths,

Florence and Chloé, for their kind and exacting proofreading,

Marianne, my sister, Candice, Lucie, and Laetitia, my friends, as well as my loved ones who were there for me during my abortion,

Mathieu, my lover, for being exactly that,

Eleven, for purring against my belly even when it was empty,

(the tiny life I've now chosen to shelter within me).

I wrote these pages between 2019 and 2022, between Lille, Ligoure, Pocé-sur-Cisse, Normandy, and Brittany, accompanied by the music of Brigitte, Anne Sylvestre, and Pomme, by the soundtracks from *The Leftovers* and *Loki*, and by the show *Inside* by Bo Burnham.

SELECTED BIBLIOGRAPHY

L'événement, Annie Ernaux, Gallimard, 2000 (*Happening*, Annie Ernaux, tr. Tanya Leslie, Seven Stories Press, 2001)

Interruption: L'avortement par celles qui l'ont vécu, Sandra Vizzavona, Stock, 2021

J'ai avorté et je vais bien, merci, Les filles des 343, La Ville Brûle, 2012 (out of print)

Il fallait que je vous le dise, Aude Mermilliod, Casterman, 2019

Ma vie sur la route, Gloria Steinem, tr. Karine Lalechère, HarperCollins, 2019 (*My Life on the Road*, Gloria Steinem, Random House, 2015)

The Turnaway Study: ten years, a thousand women, and the consequences of having — or being denied — an abortion, Diana Greene Foster, Scribner, 2020

ENDNOTES

i   Inspection Générale des Affaires Sociales, *Évaluation des
     politiques de prévention des grossesses non désirées et de prise en charge
     des interruptions volontaires de grossesse suite à la loi du 4 juillet 2001.*
     October 2009, <https://www.vie-publique.fr/sites/default/files/
     rapport/pdf/104000047.pdf>.

ii   Allyson Chiu, '"Juno" Tackled Teen Pregnancy and Abortion.
     The Woman Behind the Film Says She Wouldn't Write It
     Today,' *The Washington Post* (17 May, 2019), <https ://www.
     washingtonpost.com/nation/2019/05/17/juno-diablocody-
     georgia-alabama-abortion-bans>.

iii Emma Dibdin, '*Gilmore Girls* Has Never Been a Pro-Choice Show',
     Cosmopolitan (16 December, 2016), <https://www.cosmopolitan.
     com/entertainment/tv/a8483260/gilmore-girls-abortion.

iv   Aurélia Blanc and Alizée Vincent, '"Oui j'ai avorté." Treize
     personnalités brisent le silence', *Causette n 128*, (December 2021),
     https://www.causette.fr/feminismes/combats/temoignages-
     treize-personnalites-brisent-le-silencesur-leur-avortement.

v   Annie Ernaux, *Happening*, tr. Tanya Leslie, New York: Seven
     Stories Press, 2001.

vi Sandra Vizzavona, *Interruption: Avortement par celles qui l'ont vécu*, Stock, 2021.

vii bell hooks, *Feminism Is for Everybody: passionate politics*. South End Press, 2001.

viii Monica Davey and Joe Stumpe, 'Abortion Doctor Shot to Death in Kansas Church', *The New York Times*, 31 May 2009, <https://www.nytimes.com/2009/06/01/us/01tiller.html>.

ix Diana Greene Foster, *The Turnaway Study*, Scribner, 2020, p. 81.

x Pauline Pellissier, 'Parcours du combattant: ces Françaises, hors délai, obligées d'avorter à l'étranger', *Grazia*, 21 November 2018, <https ://www.grazia.fr/news-et-societe/societe/parcours-du-combattant-ces-francaises-hors-delai-obligees-d-avorter-a-l-etranger-908210>

xi Planning Familial, Page 'Avortement', <https://www.planningfamilial.org/fr/avortement-100>.

xii Abortion Rights Coalition of Canada, Statistics – Abortion in Canada, updated 28 March 2021, < https ://www.arcc-cdac.ca/wp-content/uploads/2020/07/statistics-abortion-in-canada.pdf>.

xiii J.D. Goodman, S. Tavernise, R. Graham, and E. Sandoval, 'Confusion in Texas as "Unprecedented" Abortion Law Takes Effect', *The New York Times*, 2 September 2021, <https ://www.nytimes.com/2021/09/02/us/supreme-court-texas-abortion-law.html>.

xiv Sébastien Natroll, 'Aux États-Unis, les femmes bientôt privées du droit constitutionnel à l'IVG ?', *Slate*, 15 December 2021, <http://www.slate.fr/story/220674/etats-unis-femmes-bientot-privees-droit-constitutionnelivg-avortement>.

xv Alexandra Jousset and Andrea Rawlins-Gaston, *Avortement, les croisés contre-attaquent*, Arte, 2017.

xvi   Jeanette Winterson, 'The Art of Fiction CL'. Interview in *The Paris Review*, n 145, Winter 1997, p. 107.

xvii   Julie Philips, 'What Contraception Meant to a Century of Women Writers', *Literary Hub*, 5 August 2019, <https ://lithub.com/whatcontraception-meant-to-a-century-of-women-writers>.

xviii Gloria Steinem, *My Life on the Road*, Random House, 2015.

xix   Ava Djamshidi, Véronique Philipponnat, and Dorothée Werner, 'Emmanuel Macron nous répond', *ELLE*, 2 July 2021.

xx   Pour une MEUF, IVG: mensonges et manipulations, le debunking de Pour une MEUF, 6 December 2020, <https://www.pourunemeuf.org/2020/12/06/ivg-mensonges-et-manipulations-le-debunking-de-pour-une-meuf>.

xxi   Statista, 'Nombre d'interruptions volontaires de grossesse (IVG) pour 1,000 femmes en France en 2018, selon la tranche d'âge', 22 November 2019, <https://fr.statista.com/statistiques/507957/nombre-d-avortements-grouped-age-femmes-France>.

xxii Diana Greene Foster, *The Turnaway Study*, Scribner, 2020, p. 24.

xxiii Diana Greene Foster, op. cit.